Tyree's Adventures

Tyree's First Day of School

Terry L. Lawrence Jr.

Edits
Carol Dean

Illustrations
Nitin Varma

YouTube
Tyree Adventures

Copyright © 2022 by Terry L. Lawrence Jr.

All rights reserved. No part of the material protected by this copyright may be reproduced or utilized in any form or by any means, electronic or mechanical, including photocopying, recording, broadcasting or by any other information storage or retrieval system, without written permission of the copyright owner unless such copying is expressly permitted by copyright law.

Tyree's dad : "Good morning, son. Are you ready for your first day of school?"

Tyree : "Yes, but I'm a little nervous, Dad."

Tyree's dad : "Being nervous is normal. There is nothing to worry about, kiddo. I bet when you get to school and see all the other kids, you won't be nervous anymore."

Tyree : "You think so?" Tyree asked.

"Tyree 's dad : Yes, son. You are going to enjoy school. Now let's brush your teeth and wash your face so you can get dressed and eat breakfast. You don't want to be late."

Tyree : "Okay, Daddy."

Tyree's dad : "How are you feeling, son?"
Tyree's : "I feel great, Dad. I'm not nervous anymore," Tyree replied.
"Dad, look at all the kids!" he shouted with excitement.
"Hey, Dad, look! Do you see that? Look, Dad, there's a big yellow bus. Hey, Da-"
"Calm down, Tyree. There's going to be a lot more exciting things that will happen today."

"Okay. Are you going to stay with me?" Tyree asked his dad.
"No, son. I have to go to work, but you know who will take care of you while I'm gone?"
"Who?"
"Your teacher," his dad replied. "Now let's find classroom twelve."
"Good morning. My name is Ms. Morton, the kindergarten teacher."
"Hello, my name is Terry, and this is my son Tyree."
"Hi, Ms. Morton," Tyree said, greeting his teacher with a big smile.
(Illustration: Dad is squatting at eye level with his son as they say their goodbyes.)
"I have to go now, son. I will be back at three o'clock to pick you up."
"Okay, Dad. I love you."
"I love you, too.". . .

"Is this mine?"

"Yes, Tyree. If you see your name on something, that means it is yours. This locker is where you will put your backpack each day."

"Good morning, class! Everyone please stand up and raise both of your hands to the sky. Now, on the count of three, I want you all to yell as loud as you can, 'I'm ready for my first day of school.' Ready?" "Yes, Ms. Morton!" the students replied.

1..2..3!!

I'm ready for my first day of school!"
"Great job, class. Our first activity today will be learning our colors. I will give each table some crayons and paper to color on."
"Great job drawing that tree, Sarah. Keep up the hard work, Kyle. And what is that you're drawing, Tyree?"

"It's a picture of me and my dad arriving at school today."
"Well, that looks great. Your dad is going to love this when he comes to pick you up."
"Thank you, Ms. Morton."
"Okay, guys, let's clean up and line up for lunch."
"It's now time for our ABC's and 1 2 3's."

"Okay, class. Your first day of school is almost over. Before you are dismissed, I want to hear how your day went. Who wants to go first?" Ms. Morton asked the students.

"Well, let's see. Eeny...meeny...miny...moe. Tyree will start us off."

"Hi, my name is Tyree, and I had a great day. I made two friends today, Sarah and Kyle. I learned a lot, too. I can't wait to come back tomorrow."

"Great job, Tyree. I'm glad you had a great first day of school. Who's next?"

"Okay, class, your parents are waiting in the hallway for you. Everyone gather your things, and I will call your name when your parent is at the door."

"Hi, Dad!" Tyree shouted, excited to see his father.
"Hey, son. Let's go home so you can tell me about your day."
"Bye, Ms. Morton. See you tomorrow," Tyree told his teacher as he waved goodbye.

"It's time for bed, Tyree. No more singing your ABC's or 123's for tonight."

"I can't help it. I just had so much fun today. I wonder what we will do tomorrow. I bet it's going to be way more fun."

"I'm glad you enjoyed your first day of school. Now let's tuck in for the night so we can be ready for tomorrow. Goodnight, son. I love you."

"Love you, too, Dad. Goodnight."

"THE END"

1. Do you remember your friend's name from school ?

_____

_____

_____

_____

2. Do you remember your first lunch at school ?

_____

_____

_____

_____

3. Write the name of your first friend and first meal at lunch.

_____

_____

_____

_____

1. Do you remember your first time playing at school with friends ?
_____
_____
_____
_____

2. Do you remember your first pair of shoes you wore to school ?
_____
_____
_____
_____

3. Write what you did when you first played at school.
_____
_____
_____
_____

1. Do you remember how you felt on your first day of school ?

___

2. Do you remember how many classmates were in your class with you?

___

3. Write how your classmates treated you ?

___

1. Do you remember how many classmates were in your class with you?

_____

_____

_____

_____

2. Write how your classmates treated you ?

_____

_____

_____

_____

Hope you enjoyed Tyree's Adventures and his First Day of School.

www.ingramcontent.com/pod-product-compliance
Lightning Source LLC
Chambersburg PA
CBHW061404010526
44119CB00010B/250